Christmas Tales & Christmas Verse by Eugene Field

Eugene Field was born on 2nd September 1850 in St. Louis, Missouri. His mother died when he was six and his father when he was nineteen. His academic life was not taken seriously and he preferred the life of a prankster until, in 1875, he began work as a journalist for the St. Joseph Gazette in Saint Joseph, Missouri.

In his career as a journalist he soon found a niche that suited him. His articles were light, humorous and written in a personal gossipy style that endeared him to his readership. Some were soon being syndicated to other newspapers around the States. Field soon rose to city editor of the Gazette.

Field had first published poetry in 1879, when his poem 'Christmas Treasures' appeared. This was the beginning that would eventually number over a dozen volumes. As well as verse Field published an extensive range of short stories including 'The Holy Cross' and 'Daniel and the Devil.'

In 1889 whilst the family were in London and Field himself was recovering from a bout of ill health he wrote his most famous poem; 'Lovers Lane'.

On 4th November 1895 Eugene Field Sr died in Chicago of a heart attack at the age of 45.

Index of Contents

IN COLORS

The angels came through the forest to where the little tree stood, and gathering around it, they touched it with their hands Frontispiece

For he was so generous that he gave away all these pretty things as fast as he made them

So Barbara fell asleep

"But why shouldn't I be merry?" asked the little mauve mouse. "To-morrow is Christmas, and this is Christmas eve"

"'What sound was that?' cried Dimas, for he was exceeding fearful"

The strange allegory of the lame boy's speech filled her with awe

But, with her babe upon her knee, Naught recked that Mother of the tree

To seek that manger out and lay Our gifts before the child— To bring our hearts and offer them Unto our King in Bethlehem!

IN BLACK-AND-WHITE

Sing, O my heart!
Sing thou in rapture this dear morn
Whereon the blessed Prince is born!

Oh, hush thee, little Dear-my-Soul,
And close thine eyes in dreaming

"This must be the house where the prince will stop," thought Barbara

Share thou this holy time with me,
The universal hymn of love

"Nestle down close, fold your hands, and shut your dear eyes!"

"They are killing me!" cried the tree

CHRISTMAS HYMN

Sing, Christmas bells!
Say to the earth this is the morn
Whereon our Savior-King is born;
Sing to all men,—the bond, the free,
The rich, the poor, the high, the low,
The little child that sports in glee,
The aged folk that tottering go,—
Proclaim the morn That Christ is born,
That saveth them and saveth me!

Sing, angel host!
Sing of the star that God has placed
Above the manger in the East;

Sing of the glories of the night,
The virgin's sweet humility,
The Babe with kingly robes bedight,—
Sing to all men where'er they be
This Christmas morn; For Christ is born,
That saveth them and saveth me!

Sing, sons of earth!
O ransomed seed of Adam, sing!
God liveth, and we have a king!
The curse is gone, the bond are free—
By Bethlehem's star that brightly beamed,
By all the heavenly signs that be,
We know that Israel is redeemed;
That on this morn The Christ is born
That saveth you and saveth me!

Sing, O my heart!
Sing thou in rapture this dear morn
Whereon the blessed Prince is born!
And as thy songs shall be of love,
So let my deeds be charity
By the dear Lord that reigns above,
By Him that died upon the tree,
By this fair morn
Whereon is born
The Christ that saveth all and me!

THE SYMBOL AND THE SAINT

Once upon a time a young man made ready for a voyage. His name was Norss; broad were his shoulders, his cheeks were ruddy, his hair was fair and long, his body betokened strength, and good-nature shone from his blue eyes and lurked about the corners of his mouth.

"Where are you going?" asked his neighbor Jans, the forge-master.

"I am going sailing for a wife," said Norss.

"For a wife, indeed!" cried Jans. "And why go you to seek her in foreign lands? Are not our maidens good enough and fair enough, that you must need search for a wife elsewhere? For shame, Norss! For shame!"

But Norss said: "A spirit came to me in my dreams last night and said, 'Launch the boat and set sail to-morrow. Have no fear; for I will guide you to the bride that awaits you.' Then, standing there, all white and beautiful, the spirit held forth a symbol—such as I had never before seen—in the figure of a cross, and the spirit said: 'By this symbol shall she be known to you.'"

"If this be so, you must need go," said Jans. "But are you well victualled? Come to my cabin, and let me give you venison and bear's meat."

Norss shook his head. "The spirit will provide," said he. "I have no fear, and I shall take no care, trusting in the spirit."

So Norss pushed his boat down the beach into the sea, and leaped into the boat, and unfurled the sail to the wind. Jans stood wondering on the beach, and watched the boat speed out of sight.

On, on, many days on sailed Norss—so many leagues that he thought he must have compassed the earth. In all this time he knew no hunger nor thirst; it was as the spirit had told him in his dream—no cares nor dangers beset him. By day the dolphins and the other creatures of the sea gambolled about his boat; by night a beauteous Star seemed to direct his course; and when he slept and dreamed, he saw ever the spirit clad in white, and holding forth to him the symbol in the similitude of a cross.

At last he came to a strange country—a country so very different from his own that he could scarcely trust his senses. Instead of the rugged mountains of the North, he saw a gentle landscape of velvety green; the trees were not pines and firs, but cypresses, cedars, and palms; instead of the cold, crisp air of his native land, he scented the perfumed zephyrs of the Orient; and the wind that filled the sail of his boat and smote his tanned cheeks was heavy and hot with the odor of cinnamon and spices. The waters were calm and blue—very different from the white and angry waves of Norss's native fiord.

As if guided by an unseen hand, the boat pointed straight for the beach of this strangely beautiful land; and ere its prow cleaved the shallower waters, Norss saw a maiden standing on the shore, shading her eyes with her right hand, and gazing intently at him. She was the most beautiful maiden he had ever looked upon. As Norss was fair, so was this maiden dark; her black hair fell loosely about her shoulders in charming contrast with the white raiment in which her slender, graceful form was clad. Around her neck she wore a golden chain, and therefrom was suspended a small symbol, which Norss did not immediately recognize.

"Hast thou come sailing out of the North into the East?" asked the maiden.

"Yes," said Norss.

"And thou art Norss?" she asked.

"I am Norss; and I come seeking my bride," he answered.

"I am she," said the maiden. "My name is Faia. An angel came to me in my dreams last night, and the angel said: 'Stand upon the beach to-day, and Norss shall come out of the North to bear thee home a bride.' So, coming here, I found thee sailing to our shore."

Remembering then the spirit's words, Norss said: "What symbol have you, Faia, that I may know how truly you have spoken?"

"No symbol have I but this," said Faia, holding out the symbol that was attached to the golden chain about her neck. Norss looked upon it, and lo! it was the symbol of his dreams,—a tiny wooden cross.

Then Norss clasped Faia in his arms and kissed her, and entering into the boat they sailed away into the North. In all their voyage neither care nor danger beset them; for as it had been told to them in their dreams, so it came to pass. By day the dolphins and the other creatures of the sea gambolled about them; by night the winds and the waves sang them to sleep; and, strangely enough, the Star which before had led Norss into the East, now shone bright and beautiful in the Northern sky!

When Norss and his bride reached their home, Jans, the forge-master, and the other neighbors made great joy, and all said that Faia was more beautiful than any other maiden in the land. So merry was Jans that he built a huge fire in his forge, and the flames thereof filled the whole Northern sky with rays of light that danced up, up, up to the Star, singing glad songs the while. So Norss and Faia were wed, and they went to live in the cabin in the fir grove.

To these two was born in good time a son, whom they named Claus. On the night that he was born wondrous things came to pass. To the cabin in the fir grove came all the quaint, weird spirits,—the fairies, the elves, the trolls, the pixies, the fadas, the crions, the goblins, the kobolds, the moss-people, the gnomes, the dwarfs, the water-sprites, the courils, the bogles, the brownies, the nixies, the trows, the stille-volk,—all came to the cabin in the fir grove, and capered about and sang the strange, beautiful songs of the Mist-Land. And the flames of old Jans's forge leaped up higher than ever into the Northern sky, carrying the joyous tidings to the Star, and full of music was that happy night.

Even in infancy Claus did marvellous things. With his baby hands he wrought into pretty figures the willows that were given him to play with. As he grew older, he fashioned, with the knife old Jans had made for him, many curious toys,—carts, horses, dogs, lambs, houses, trees, cats, and birds, all of wood and very like to nature. His mother taught him how to make dolls too,—dolls of every kind, condition, temper, and color; proud dolls, homely dolls, boy dolls, lady dolls, wax dolls, rubber dolls, paper dolls, worsted dolls, rag dolls,—dolls of every description and without end. So Claus became at once quite as popular with the little girls as with the little boys of his native village; for he was so generous that he gave away all these pretty things as fast as he made them.

Claus seemed to know by instinct every language. As he grew older he would ramble off into the woods and talk with the trees, the rocks, and the beasts of the greenwood; or he would sit on the cliffs overlooking the fiord, and listen to the stories that the waves of the sea loved to tell him; then, too, he knew the haunts of the elves and the stille-volk, and many a pretty tale he learned from these little people. When night came, old Jans told him the quaint legends of the North, and his mother sang to him the lullabies she had heard when a little child herself in the far-distant East. And every night his mother held out to him the symbol in the similitude of the cross, and bade him kiss it ere he went to sleep.

So Claus grew to manhood, increasing each day in knowledge and in wisdom. His works increased too; and his liberality dispensed everywhere the beauteous things which his fancy conceived and his skill executed. Jans, being now a very old man, and having no son of his own, gave to Claus his forge and workshop, and taught him those secret arts which he in youth had learned from cunning masters. Right joyous now was Claus; and many, many times the Northern sky glowed with the flames that danced singing from the forge while Claus moulded his pretty toys. Every color of the rainbow were these flames; for they reflected the bright colors of the beauteous things strewn round that wonderful workshop. Just as of old he had dispensed to all children alike the homelier toys of his youth, so now he gave to all children alike these more beautiful and more curious gifts. So little children everywhere loved Claus, because he gave them pretty toys, and their parents loved him because he made their little ones so happy.

But now Norss and Faia were come to old age. After long years of love and happiness, they knew that death could not be far distant. And one day Faia said to Norss: "Neither you nor I, dear love, fear death; but if we could choose, would we not choose to live always in this our son Claus, who has been so sweet a joy to us?"

"Ay, ay," said Norss; "but how is that possible?"

"We shall see," said Faia.

That night Norss dreamed that a spirit came to him, and that the spirit said to him: "Norss, thou shalt surely live forever in thy son Claus, if thou wilt but acknowledge the symbol."

Then when the morning was come Norss told his dream to Faia, his wife; and Faia said:

"The same dream had I,—an angel appearing to me and speaking these very words."

"But what of the symbol?" cried Norss.

"I have it here, about my neck," said Faia.

So saying, Faia drew from her bosom the symbol of wood,—a tiny cross suspended about her neck by the golden chain. And as she stood there holding the symbol out to Norss, he—he thought of the time when first he saw her on the far-distant Orient shore, standing beneath the Star in all her maidenly glory, shading her beauteous eyes with one hand, and with the other clasping the cross,—the holy talisman of her faith.

"Faia, Faia!" cried Norss, "it is the same,—the same you wore when I fetched you a bride from the East!"

"It is the same," said Faia, "yet see how my kisses and my prayers have worn it away; for many, many times in these years, dear Norss, have I pressed it to my lips and breathed your name upon it. See now—see what a beauteous light its shadow makes upon your aged face!"

The sunbeams, indeed, streaming through the window at that moment, cast the shadow of the symbol on old Norss's brow. Norss felt a glorious warmth suffuse him, his heart leaped with joy, and he stretched out his arms and fell about Faia's neck, and kissed the symbol and acknowledged it. Then likewise did Faia; and suddenly the place was filled with a wondrous brightness and with strange music, and never thereafter were Norss and Faia beholden of men.

Until late that night Claus toiled at his forge; for it was a busy season with him, and he had many, many curious and beauteous things to make for the little children in the country round about. The colored flames leaped singing from his forge, so that the Northern sky seemed to be lighted by a thousand rainbows; but above all this voiceful glory beamed the Star, bright, beautiful, serene.

Coming late to the cabin in the fir grove, Claus wondered that no sign of his father or of his mother was to be seen. "Father—mother!" he cried, but he received no answer. Just then the Star cast its golden gleam through the latticed window, and this strange, holy light fell and rested upon the symbol of the cross that lay upon the floor. Seeing it, Claus stooped and picked it up, and kissing it reverently, he cried: "Dear talisman, be thou my inspiration evermore; and wheresoever thy blessed influence is felt, there also let my works be known henceforth forever!"

No sooner had he said these words than Claus felt the gift of immortality bestowed upon him; and in that moment, too, there came to him a knowledge that his parents' prayer had been answered, and that Norss and Faia would live in him through all time.

And lo! to that place and in that hour came all the people of Mist-Land and of Dream-Land to declare allegiance to him: yes, the elves, the fairies, the pixies,—all came to Claus, prepared to do his bidding. Joyously they capered about him, and merrily they sang.

"Now haste ye all," cried Claus,—"haste ye all to your homes and bring to my workshop the best ye have. Search, little hill-people, deep in the bowels of the earth for finest gold and choicest jewels; fetch me, O mermaids, from the bottom of the sea the treasures hidden there,—the shells of rainbow tints, the smooth, bright pebbles, and the strange ocean flowers; go, pixies, and other water-sprites, to your secret lakes, and bring me pearls! Speed! speed you all! for many pretty things have we to make for the little ones of earth we love!"

But to the kobolds and the brownies Claus said: "Fly to every house on earth where the cross is known; loiter unseen in the corners, and watch and hear the children through the day. Keep a strict account of good and bad, and every night bring back to me the names of good and bad that I may know them."

The kobolds and the brownies laughed gleefully, and sped away on noiseless wings; and so, too, did the other fairies and elves.

There came also to Claus the beasts of the forest and the birds of the air, and bade him be their master. And up danced the Four Winds, and they said: "May we not serve you, too?"

The Snow King came stealing along in his feathery chariot. "Oho!" he cried, "I shall speed over all the world and tell them you are coming. In town and country, on the mountain-tops and in the valleys,—wheresoever the cross is raised,—there will I herald your approach, and thither will I strew you a pathway of feathery white. Oho! oho!" So, singing softly, the Snow King stole upon his way.

But of all the beasts that begged to do him service, Claus liked the reindeer best. "You shall go with me in my travels; for henceforth I shall bear my treasures not only to the children of the North, but to the children in every land whither the Star points me and where the cross is lifted up!" So said Claus to the reindeer, and the reindeer neighed joyously and stamped their hoofs impatiently, as though they longed to start immediately.

Oh, many, many times has Claus whirled away from his far Northern home in his sledge drawn by the reindeer, and thousands upon thousands of beautiful gifts—all of his own making—has he borne to the children of every land; for he loves them all alike, and they all alike love him, I trow. So truly do they love him that they call him Santa Claus, and I am sure that he must be a saint; for he has lived these many hundred years, and we, who know that he was born of Faith and Love, believe that he will live forever.

CHRISTMAS EVE

Oh, hush thee, little Dear-my-Soul,
The evening shades are falling,—
Hush thee, my dear, dost thou not hear

The voice of the Master calling?

Deep lies the snow upon the earth,
But all the sky is ringing
With joyous song, and all night long
The stars shall dance, with singing.

Oh, hush thee, little Dear-my-Soul,
And close thine eyes in dreaming,
And angels fair shall lead thee where
The singing stars are beaming.

A shepherd calls his little lambs,
And he longeth to caress them;
He bids them rest upon his breast,
That his tender love may bless them.

So, hush thee, little Dear-my-Soul,
Whilst evening shades are falling,
And above the song of the heavenly throng
Thou shalt hear the Master calling.

JOEL'S TALK WITH SANTA CLAUS

One Christmas eve Joel Baker was in a most unhappy mood. He was lonesome and miserable; the chimes making merry Christmas music outside disturbed rather than soothed him, the jingle of the sleigh-bells fretted him, and the shrill whistling of the wind around the corners of the house and up and down the chimney seemed to grate harshly on his ears.

"Humph," said Joel, wearily, "Christmas is nothin' to me; there was a time when it meant a great deal, but that was long ago—fifty years is a long stretch to look back over. There is nothin' in Christmas now, nothin' for me at least; it is so long since Santa Claus remembered me that I venture to say he has forgotten that there ever was such a person as Joel Baker in all the world. It used to be different; Santa Claus used to think a great deal of me when I was a boy. Ah! Christmas nowadays ain't what it was in the good old time—no, not what it used to be."

As Joel was absorbed in his distressing thoughts he became aware very suddenly that somebody was entering or trying to enter the room. First came a draught of cold air, then a scraping, grating sound, then a strange shuffling, and then,—yes, then, all at once, Joel saw a pair of fat legs and a still fatter body dangle down the chimney, followed presently by a long white beard, above which appeared a jolly red nose and two bright twinkling eyes, while over the head and forehead was drawn a fur cap, white with snowflakes.

"Ha, ha," chuckled the fat, jolly stranger, emerging from the chimney and standing well to one side of the hearth-stone; "ha, ha, they don't have the big, wide chimneys they used to build, but they can't keep Santa Claus out—no, they can't keep Santa Claus out! Ha, ha, ha. Though the chimney were no bigger than a gas pipe, Santa Claus would slide down it!"

It didn't require a second glance to assure Joel that the new-comer was indeed Santa Claus. Joel knew the good old saint—oh, yes—and he had seen him once before, and, although that was when Joel was a little boy, he had never forgotten how Santa Claus looked.

Nor had Santa Claus forgotten Joel, although Joel thought he had; for now Santa Claus looked kindly at Joel and smiled and said: "Merry Christmas to you, Joel!"

"Thank you, old Santa Claus," replied Joel, "but I don't believe it's going to be a very merry Christmas. It's been so long since I've had a merry Christmas that I don't believe I'd know how to act if I had one."

"Let's see," said Santa Claus, "it must be going on fifty years since I saw you last—yes, you were eight years old the last time I slipped down the chimney of the old homestead and filled your stocking. Do you remember it?"

"I remember it well," answered Joel. "I had made up my mind to lie awake and see Santa Claus; I had heard tell of you, but I'd never seen you, and Brother Otis and I concluded we'd lie awake and watch for you to come."

Santa Claus shook his head reproachfully.

"That was very wrong," said he, "for I'm so scarey that if I'd known you boys were awake I'd never have come down the chimney at all, and then you'd have had no presents."

"But Otis couldn't keep awake," explained Joel. "We talked about everythin' we could think of, till father called out to us that if we didn't stop talking he'd have to send one of us up into the attic to sleep with the hired man. So in less than five minutes Otis was sound asleep and no pinching could wake him up. But I was bound to see Santa Claus and I don't believe anything would've put me to sleep. I heard the big clock in the sitting-room strike eleven, and I had begun wonderin' if you never were going to come, when all of a sudden I heard the tinkle of the bells around your reindeers' necks. Then I heard the reindeers prancin' on the roof and the sound of your sleigh-runners cuttin' through the crust and slippin' over the shingles. I was kind o' scared and I covered my head up with the sheet and quilts—only I left a little hole so I could peek out and see what was goin' on. As soon as I saw you I got over bein' scared—for you were jolly and smilin' like, and you chuckled as you went around to each stockin' and filled it up."

"Yes, I can remember the night," said Santa Claus. "I brought you a sled, didn't I?"

"Yes, and you brought Otis one, too," replied Joel. "Mine was red and had 'Yankee Doodle' painted in black letters on the side; Otis's was black and had 'Snow Queen' in gilt letters."

"I remember those sleds distinctly," said Santa Claus, "for I made them specially for you boys."

"You set the sleds up against the wall," continued Joel, "and then you filled the stockin's."

"There were six of 'em, as I recollect?" said Santa Claus.

"Let me see," queried Joel. "There was mine, and Otis's, and Elvira's, and Thankful's, and Susan Prickett's—Susan was our help, you know. No, there were only five, and, as I remember, they were the biggest we could beg or borrer of Aunt Dorcas, who weighed nigh unto two hundred pounds. Otis and I didn't like Susan Prickett, and we were hopin' you'd put a cold potato in her stockin'."

"But Susan was a good girl," remonstrated Santa Claus. "You know I put cold potatoes only in the stockin's of boys and girls who are bad and don't believe in Santa Claus."

"At any rate," said Joel, "you filled all the stockin's with candy and pop-corn and nuts and raisins, and I can remember you said you were afraid you'd run out of pop-corn balls before you got around. Then you left each of us a book. Elvira got the best one, which was 'The Garland of Frien'ship,' and had poems in it about the bleeding of hearts, and so forth. Father wasn't expectin' anything, but you left him a new pair of mittens, and mother got a new fur boa to wear to meetin'."

"Of course," said Santa Claus, "I never forgot father and mother."

"Well, it was as much as I could do to lay still," continued Joel, "for I'd been longin' for a sled, an' the sight of that red sled with 'Yankee Doodle' painted on it jest made me wild. But, somehow or other, I began to get powerful sleepy all at once, and I couldn't keep my eyes open. The next thing I knew Otis was nudgin' me in the ribs. 'Git up, Joel,' says he; 'it's Chris'mas an' Santa Claus has been here.' 'Merry Chris'mas! Merry Chris'mas!' we cried as we tumbled out o' bed. Then Elvira an' Thankful came in, not more 'n half dressed, and Susan came in, too, an' we just made Rome howl with 'Merry Chris'mas! Merry Chris'mas!' to each other. 'Ef you children don't make less noise in there,' cried father, 'I'll hev to send you all back to bed.' The idea of askin' boys an' girls to keep quiet on Chris'mas mornin' when they've got new sleds an' 'Garlands of Frien'ship'!"

Santa Claus chuckled; his rosy cheeks fairly beamed joy.

"Otis an' I didn't want any breakfast," said Joel. "We made up our minds that a stockin'ful of candy and pop-corn and raisins would stay us for a while. I do believe there wasn't buckwheat cakes enough in the township to keep us indoors that mornin'; buckwheat cakes don't size up much 'longside of a red sled with 'Yankee Doodle' painted onto it and a black sled named 'Snow Queen.' We didn't care how cold it was—so much the better for slidin' downhill! All the boys had new sleds—Lafe Dawson, Bill Holbrook, Gum Adams, Rube Playford, Leander Merrick, Ezra Purple—all on 'em had new sleds excep' Martin Peavey, and he said he calculated Santa Claus had skipped him this year 'cause his father had broke his leg haulin' logs from the Pelham woods and had been kep' indoors six weeks. But Martin had his ol' sled, and he didn't hev to ask any odds of any of us, neither."

"I brought Martin a sled the next Christmas," said Santa Claus.

"Like as not—but did you ever slide downhill, Santa Claus? I don't mean such hills as they hev out here in this new country, but one of them old-fashioned New England hills that was made 'specially for boys to slide down, full of bumpers an' thank-ye-marms, and about ten times longer comin' up than it is goin' down! The wind blew in our faces and almos' took our breath away. 'Merry Chris'mas to ye, little boys!' it seemed to say, and it untied our mufflers an' whirled the snow in our faces, jist as if it was a boy, too, an' wanted to play with us. An ol' crow came flappin' over us from the cornfield beyond the meadow. He said: 'Caw, caw,' when he saw my new sled—I s'pose he'd never seen a red one before. Otis had a hard time with his sled—the black one—an' he wondered why it wouldn't go as fast as mine would. 'Hev you scraped the paint off'n the runners?' asked Wralsey Goodnow. 'Course I hev,' said Otis; 'broke my own knife an' Lute Ingraham's a-doin' it, but it don't seem to make no dif'rence—the darned ol' thing won't go!' Then, what did Simon Buzzell say but that, like's not, it was because Otis's sled's name was 'Snow Queen.' 'Never did see a girl sled that was worth a cent, anyway,' sez Simon. Well, now, that jest about broke Otis up in business. 'It ain't a girl sled,' sez he, 'and its name ain't "Snow Queen"! I'm a-goin' to call it "Dan'l Webster," or "Ol'ver

Optic," or "Sheriff Robbins," or after some other big man!' An' the boys plagued him so much about that pesky girl sled that he scratched off the name, an', as I remember, it did go better after that!

"About the only thing," continued Joel, "that marred the harmony of the occasion, as the editor of the Hampshire County Phoenix used to say, was the ashes that Deacon Morris Frisbie sprinkled out in front of his house. He said he wasn't going to have folks breakin' their necks jest on account of a lot of frivolous boys that was goin' to the gallows as fas' as they could! Oh, how we hated him! and we'd have snowballed him, too, if we hadn't been afraid of the constable that lived next door. But the ashes didn't bother us much, and every time we slid side-saddle we'd give the ashes a kick, and that sort of scattered 'em."

The bare thought of this made Santa Claus laugh.

"Goin' on about nine o'clock," said Joel, "the girls come along—Sister Elvira an' Thankful, Prudence Tucker, Belle Yocum, Sophrone Holbrook, Sis Hubbard, an' Marthy Sawyer. Marthy's brother Increase wanted her to ride on his sled, but Marthy allowed that a red sled was her choice every time. 'I don't see how I'm goin' to hold on,' said Marthy. 'Seems as if I would hev my hands full keepin' my things from blowin' away.' 'Don't worry about yourself, Marthy,' sez I, 'for if you'll look after your things, I kind o' calc'late I'll manage not to lose you on the way.' Dear Marthy—seems as if I could see you now, with your tangled hair a-blowin' in the wind, your eyes all bright and sparklin', an' your cheeks as red as apples. Seems, too, as if I could hear you laughin' and callin', jist as you did as I toiled up the old New England hill that Chris'mas mornin'—a-callin': 'Joel, Joel, Joel—ain't ye ever comin', Joel?' But the hill is long and steep, Marthy, an' Joel ain't the boy he used to be; he's old, an' gray, an' feeble, but there's love an' faith in his heart, an' they kind o' keep him totterin' tow'rd the voice he hears a-callin': 'Joel, Joel, Joel!'"

"I know—I see it all," murmured Santa Claus very softly.

"Oh, that was so long ago," sighed Joel; "so very long ago! And I've had no Chris'mas since—only once, when our little one—Marthy's an' mine—you remember him, Santa Claus?"

"Yes," said Santa Claus, "a toddling little boy with blue eyes—"

"Like his mother," interrupted Joel; "an' he was like her, too—so gentle an' lovin', only we called him Joel, for that was my father's name and it kind o' run in the fam'ly. He wa'n't more'n three years old when you came with your Chris'mas presents for him, Santa Claus. We had told him about you, and he used to go to the chimney every night and make a little prayer about what he wanted you to bring him. And you brought 'em, too—a stick-horse, an' a picture-book, an' some blocks, an' a drum—they're on the shelf in the closet there, and his little Chris'mas stockin' with 'em—I've saved 'em all, an' I've taken 'em down an' held 'em in my hands, oh, so many times!"

"But when I came again," said Santa Claus—

"His little bed was empty, an' I was alone. It killed his mother—Marthy was so tender-hearted; she kind o' drooped an' pined after that. So now they've been asleep side by side in the buryin'-ground these thirty years.

"That's why I'm so sad-like whenever Chris'mas comes," said Joel, after a pause. "The thinkin' of long ago makes me bitter almost. It's so different now from what it used to be."

"No, Joel, oh, no," said Santa Claus. "'Tis the same world, and human nature is the same and always will be. But Christmas is for the little folks, and you, who are old and grizzled now, must know it and love it only through the gladness it brings the little ones."

"True," groaned Joel; "but how may I know and feel this gladness when I have no little stocking hanging in my chimney corner—no child to please me with his prattle? See, I am alone."

"No, you're not alone, Joel," said Santa Claus. "There are children in this great city who would love and bless you for your goodness if you but touched their hearts. Make them happy, Joel; send by me this night some gift to the little boy in the old house yonder—he is poor and sick; a simple toy will fill his Christmas with gladness."

"His little sister, too—take her some presents," said Joel; "make them happy for me, Santa Claus—you are right—make them happy for me."

How sweetly Joel slept! When he awoke, the sunlight streamed in through the window and seemed to bid him a merry Christmas. How contented and happy Joel felt! It must have been the talk with Santa Claus that did it all; he had never known a sweeter sense of peace. A little girl came out of the house over the way. She had a new doll in her arms, and she sang a merry little song and she laughed with joy as she skipped along the street. Ay, and at the window sat the little sick boy, and the toy Santa Claus left him seemed to have brought him strength and health, for his eyes sparkled and his cheeks glowed, and it was plain to see his heart was full of happiness.

And, oh! how the chimes did ring out, and how joyfully they sang their Christmas carol that morning! They sang of Bethlehem and the manger and the Babe; they sang of love and charity, till all the Christmas air seemed full of angel voices.

Carol of the Christmas morn— Carol of the Christ-child born— Carol to the list'ning sky Till it echoes back again "Glory be to God on high, Peace on earth, good will tow'rd men!"

So all this music—the carol of the chimes, the sound of children's voices, the smile of the poor little boy over the way—all this sweet music crept into Joel's heart that Christmas morning; yes, and with these sweet, holy influences came others so subtile and divine that in its silent communion with them, Joel's heart cried out amen and amen to the glory of the Christmas time.

THE THREE KINGS OF COLOGNE

From out Cologne there came three kings
To worship Jesus Christ, their King.
To Him they sought fine herbs they brought,
And many a beauteous golden thing;
They brought their gifts to Bethlehem town,
And in that manger set them down.

Then spake the first king, and he said:
"O Child, most heavenly, bright, and fair!
I bring this crown to Bethlehem town
For Thee, and only Thee, to wear;
So give a heavenly crown to me

When I shall come at last to Thee!"

The second, then. "I bring Thee here
This royal robe, O Child!" he cried;
"Of silk 'tis spun, and such an one
There is not in the world beside;
So in the day of doom requite
Me with a heavenly robe of white!"

The third king gave his gift, and quoth:
"Spikenard and myrrh to Thee I bring,
And with these twain would I most fain
Anoint the body of my King;
So may their incense sometime rise
To plead for me in yonder skies!"

Thus spake the three kings of Cologne,
That gave their gifts, and went their way;
And now kneel I in prayer hard by
The cradle of the Child to-day;
Nor crown, nor robe, nor spice I bring
As offering unto Christ, my King.

Yet have I brought a gift the Child
May not despise, however small;
For here I lay my heart to-day,
And it is full of love to all.
Take Thou the poor but loyal thing,
My only tribute, Christ, my King!

THE COMING OF THE PRINCE

I

"Whirr-r-r! whirr-r-r! whirr-r-r!" said the wind, and it tore through the streets of the city that Christmas eve, turning umbrellas inside out, driving the snow in fitful gusts before it, creaking the rusty signs and shutters, and playing every kind of rude prank it could think of.

"How cold your breath is to-night!" said Barbara, with a shiver, as she drew her tattered little shawl the closer around her benumbed body.

"Whirr-r-r! whirr-r-r! whirr-r-r!" answered the wind; "but why are you out in this storm? You should be at home by the warm fire."

"I have no home," said Barbara; and then she sighed bitterly, and something like a tiny pearl came in the corner of one of her sad blue eyes.

But the wind did not hear her answer, for it had hurried up the street to throw a handful of snow in the face of an old man who was struggling along with a huge basket of good things on each arm.

"Why are you not at the cathedral?" asked a snowflake, as it alighted on Barbara's shoulder. "I heard grand music, and saw beautiful lights there as I floated down from the sky a moment ago."

"What are they doing at the cathedral?" inquired Barbara.

"Why, haven't you heard?" exclaimed the snowflake. "I supposed everybody knew that the prince was coming to-morrow."

"Surely enough; this is Christmas eve," said Barbara, "and the prince will come to-morrow."

Barbara remembered that her mother had told her about the prince, how beautiful and good and kind and gentle he was, and how he loved the little children; but her mother was dead now, and there was none to tell Barbara of the prince and his coming,—none but the little snowflake.

"I should like to see the prince," said Barbara, "for I have heard he was very beautiful and good."

"That he is," said the snowflake. "I have never seen him, but I heard the pines and the firs singing about him as I floated over the forest to-night."

"Whirr-r-r! whirr-r-r!" cried the wind, returning boisterously to where Barbara stood. "I've been looking for you everywhere, little snowflake! So come with me."

And without any further ado, the wind seized upon the snowflake and hurried it along the street and led it a merry dance through the icy air of the winter night.

Barbara trudged on through the snow and looked in at the bright things in the shop windows. The glitter of the lights and the sparkle of the vast array of beautiful Christmas toys quite dazzled her. A strange mingling of admiration, regret, and envy filled the poor little creature's heart.

"Much as I may yearn to have them, it cannot be," she said to herself, "yet I may feast my eyes upon them."

"Go away from here!" said a harsh voice. "How can the rich people see all my fine things if you stand before the window? Be off with you, you miserable little beggar!"

It was the shopkeeper, and he gave Barbara a savage box on the ear that sent her reeling into the deeper snowdrifts of the gutter.

Presently she came to a large house where there seemed to be much mirth and festivity. The shutters were thrown open, and through the windows Barbara could see a beautiful Christmas-tree in the centre of a spacious room—a beautiful Christmas-tree ablaze with red and green lights, and heavy with toys and stars and glass balls and other beautiful things that children love. There was a merry throng around the tree, and the children were smiling and gleeful, and all in that house seemed content and happy. Barbara heard them singing, and their song was about the prince who was to come on the morrow.

"This must be the house where the prince will stop," thought Barbara. "How I would like to see his face and hear his voice!—yet what would he care for me, a 'miserable little beggar'?"

So Barbara crept on through the storm, shivering and disconsolate, yet thinking of the prince.

"Where are you going?" she asked of the wind as it overtook her.

"To the cathedral," laughed the wind. "The great people are flocking there, and I will have a merry time amongst them, ha, ha, ha!"

And with laughter the wind whirled away and chased the snow toward the cathedral.

"It is there, then, that the prince will come," thought Barbara. "It is a beautiful place, and the people will pay him homage there. Perhaps I shall see him if I go there."

So she went to the cathedral. Many folk were there in their richest apparel, and the organ rolled out its grand music, and the people sang wondrous songs, and the priests made eloquent prayers; and the music, and the songs, and the prayers were all about the prince and his expected coming. The throng that swept in and out of the great edifice talked always of the prince, the prince, the prince, until Barbara really loved him very much, for all the gentle words she heard the people say of him.

"Please, can I go and sit inside?" inquired Barbara of the sexton.

"No!" said the sexton gruffly, for this was an important occasion with the sexton, and he had no idea of wasting words on a beggar child.

"But I will be very good and quiet," pleaded Barbara. "Please may I not see the prince?"

"I have said no, and I mean it," retorted the sexton. "What have you for the prince, or what cares the prince for you? Out with you, and don't be blocking up the door-way!" So the sexton gave Barbara an angry push, and the child fell half-way down the icy steps of the cathedral. She began to cry. Some great people were entering the cathedral at the time, and they laughed to see her falling.

"Have you seen the prince?" inquired a snowflake, alighting on Barbara's cheek. It was the same little snowflake that had clung to her shawl an hour ago, when the wind came galloping along on his boisterous search.

"Ah, no!" sighed Barbara in tears; "but what cares the prince for me?"

"Do not speak so bitterly," said the little snowflake. "Go to the forest and you shall see him, for the prince always comes through the forest to the city."

Despite the cold, and her bruises, and her tears, Barbara smiled. In the forest she could behold the prince coming on his way; and he would not see her, for she would hide among the trees and vines.

"Whirr-r-r, whirr-r-r!" It was the mischievous, romping wind once more; and it fluttered Barbara's tattered shawl, and set her hair to streaming in every direction, and swept the snowflake from her cheek and sent it spinning through the air.

Barbara trudged toward the forest. When she came to the city gate the watchman stopped her, and held his big lantern in her face, and asked her who she was and where she was going.

"I am Barbara, and I am going into the forest," said she boldly.

"Into the forest?" cried the watchman, "and in this storm? No, child; you will perish!"

"But I am going to see the prince," said Barbara. "They will not let me watch for him in the church, nor in any of their pleasant homes, so I am going into the forest."

The watchman smiled sadly. He was a kindly man; he thought of his own little girl at home.

"No, you must not go to the forest," said he, "for you would perish with the cold."

But Barbara would not stay. She avoided the watchman's grasp and ran as fast as ever she could through the city gate.

"Come back, come back!" cried the watchman; "you will perish in the forest!"

But Barbara would not heed his cry. The falling snow did not stay her, nor did the cutting blast. She thought only of the prince, and she ran straightway to the forest.

II

"What do you see up there, O pine-tree?" asked a little vine in the forest. "You lift your head among the clouds to-night, and you tremble strangely as if you saw wondrous sights."

"I see only the distant hill-tops and the dark clouds," answered the pine-tree. "And the wind sings of the snow-king to-night; to all my questionings he says, 'Snow, snow, snow,' till I am wearied with his refrain."

"But the prince will surely come to-morrow?" inquired the tiny snowdrop that nestled close to the vine.

"Oh, yes," said the vine. "I heard the country folks talking about it as they went through the forest to-day, and they said that the prince would surely come on the morrow."

"What are you little folks down there talking about?" asked the pine-tree.

"We are talking about the prince," said the vine.

"Yes, he is to come on the morrow," said the pine-tree, "but not until the day dawns, and it is still all dark in the east."

"Yes," said the fir-tree, "the east is black, and only the wind and the snow issue from it."

"Keep your head out of my way!" cried the pine-tree to the fir; "with your constant bobbing around I can hardly see at all."

"Take that for your bad manners," retorted the fir, slapping the pine-tree savagely with one of her longest branches.

The pine-tree would put up with no such treatment, so he hurled his largest cone at the fir; and for a moment or two it looked as if there were going to be a serious commotion in the forest.

"Hush!" cried the vine in a startled tone; "there is some one coming through the forest."

The pine-tree and the fir stopped quarrelling, and the snowdrop nestled closer to the vine, while the vine hugged the pine-tree very tightly. All were greatly alarmed.

"Nonsense!" said the pine-tree, in a tone of assumed bravery. "No one would venture into the forest at such an hour."

"Indeed! and why not?" cried a child's voice. "Will you not let me watch with you for the coming of the prince?"

"Will you not chop me down?" inquired the pine-tree gruffly.

"Will you not tear me from my tree?" asked the vine.

"Will you not pluck my blossoms?" plaintively piped the snowdrop.

"No, of course not," said Barbara; "I have come only to watch with you for the prince."

Then Barbara told them who she was, and how cruelly she had been treated in the city, and how she longed to see the prince, who was to come on the morrow. And as she talked, the forest and all therein felt a great compassion for her.

"Lie at my feet," said the pine-tree, "and I will protect you."

"Nestle close to me, and I will chafe your temples and body and limbs till they are warm," said the vine.

"Let me rest upon your cheek, and I will sing you my little songs," said the snowdrop.

And Barbara felt very grateful for all these homely kindnesses. She rested in the velvety snow at the foot of the pine-tree, and the vine chafed her body and limbs, and the little flower sang sweet songs to her.

"Whirr-r-r, whirr-r-r!" There was that noisy wind again, but this time it was gentler than it had been in the city.

"Here you are, my little Barbara," said the wind, in kindly tones. "I have brought you the little snowflake. I am glad you came away from the city, for the people are proud and haughty there; oh, but I will have my fun with them!"

Then, having dropped the little snowflake on Barbara's cheek, the wind whisked off to the city again. And we can imagine that it played rare pranks with the proud, haughty folk on its return; for the wind, as you know, is no respecter of persons.

"Dear Barbara," said the snowflake, "I will watch with thee for the coming of the prince."

And Barbara was glad, for she loved the little snowflake, that was so pure and innocent and gentle.

"Tell us, O pine-tree," cried the vine, "what do you see in the east? Has the prince yet entered the forest?"

"The east is full of black clouds," said the pine-tree, "and the winds that hurry to the hill-tops sing of the snow."

"But the city is full of brightness," said the fir. "I can see the lights in the cathedral, and I can hear wondrous music about the prince and his coming."

"Yes, they are singing of the prince in the cathedral," said Barbara sadly.

"But we shall see him first," whispered the vine reassuringly.

"Yes, the prince will come through the forest," said the little snowdrop gleefully.

"Fear not, dear Barbara, we shall behold the prince in all his glory," cried the snowflake.

Then all at once there was a strange hub-bub in the forest; for it was midnight, and the spirits came from their hiding-places to prowl about and to disport themselves. Barbara beheld them all in great wonder and trepidation, for she had never before seen the spirits of the forest, although she had often heard of them. It was a marvellous sight.

"Fear nothing," whispered the vine to Barbara,—"fear nothing, for they dare not touch you."

The antics of the wood-spirits continued but an hour; for then a cock crowed, and immediately thereat, with a wondrous scurrying, the elves and the gnomes and the other grotesque spirits sought their abiding-places in the caves and in the hollow trunks and under the loose bark of the trees. And then it was very quiet once more in the forest.

"It is very cold," said Barbara. "My hands and feet are like ice."

Then the pine-tree and the fir shook down the snow from their broad boughs, and the snow fell upon Barbara and covered her like a white mantle.

"You will be warm now," said the vine, kissing Barbara's forehead. And Barbara smiled.

Then the snowdrop sang a lullaby about the moss that loved the violet. And Barbara said, "I am going to sleep; will you wake me when the prince comes through the forest?"

And they said they would. So Barbara fell asleep.

III

"The bells in the city are ringing merrily," said the fir, "and the music in the cathedral is louder and more beautiful than before. Can it be that the prince has already come into the city?"

"No," cried the pine-tree, "look to the east and see the Christmas day a-dawning! The prince is coming, and his pathway is through the forest!"

The storm had ceased. Snow lay upon all the earth. The hills, the forest, the city, and the meadows were white with the robe the storm-king had thrown over them. Content with his wondrous work, the storm-king himself had fled to his far Northern home before the dawn of the Christmas day. Everything was bright and sparkling and beautiful. And most beautiful was the great hymn of praise the forest sang that Christmas morning,—the pine-trees and the firs and the vines and the snow-flowers that sang of the prince and of his promised coming.

"Wake up, little one," cried the vine, "for the prince is coming!"

But Barbara slept; she did not hear the vine's soft calling nor the lofty music of the forest.

A little snow-bird flew down from the fir-tree's bough and perched upon the vine, and carolled in Barbara's ear of the Christmas morning and of the coming of the prince. But Barbara slept; she did not hear the carol of the bird.

"Alas!" sighed the vine, "Barbara will not awaken, and the prince is coming."

Then the vine and the snowdrop wept, and the pine-tree and the fir were very sad.

The prince came through the forest clad in royal raiment and wearing a golden crown. Angels came with him, and the forest sang a great hymn unto the prince, such a hymn as had never before been heard on earth. The prince came to the sleeping child and smiled upon her and called her by name.

"Barbara, my little one," said the prince, "awaken, and come with me."

Then Barbara opened her eyes and beheld the prince. And it seemed as if a new life had come to her, for there was warmth in her body and a flush upon her cheeks and a light in her eyes that were divine. And she was clothed no longer in rags, but in white flowing raiment; and upon the soft brown hair there was a crown like those which angels wear. And as Barbara arose and went to the prince, the little snowflake fell from her cheek upon her bosom, and forthwith became a pearl more precious than all other jewels upon earth.

And the prince took Barbara in his arms and blessed her, and turning round about, returned with the little child unto his home, while the forest and the sky and the angels sang a wondrous song.

The city waited for the prince, but he did not come. None knew of the glory of the forest that Christmas morning, nor of the new life that came to little Barbara.

Come thou, dear Prince, oh, come to us this holy Christmas time! Come to the busy marts of earth, the quiet homes, the noisy streets, the humble lanes; come to us all, and with thy love touch every human heart, that we may know that love, and in its blessed peace bear charity to all mankind!

CHRYSTMASSE OF OLDE

God rest you, Chrysten gentil men,
Wherever you may be,—
God rest you all in fielde or hall,
Or on ye stormy sea;
For on this morn oure Chryst is born
That saveth you and me.

Last night ye shepherds in ye east
Saw many a wondrous thing;

Ye sky last night flamed passing bright
Whiles that ye stars did sing,
And angels came to bless ye name
Of Jesus Chryst, oure Kyng.

God rest you, Chrysten gentil men,
Faring where'er you may;
In noblesse court do thou no sport,
In tournament no playe,
In paynim lands hold thou thy hands
From bloudy works this daye.

But thinking on ye gentil Lord
That died upon ye tree,
Let troublings cease and deeds of peace
Abound in Chrystantie;
For on this morn ye Chryst is born
That saveth you and me.

THE MOUSE AND THE MOONBEAM

Whilst you were sleeping, little Dear-my-Soul, strange things happened; but that I saw and heard them, I should never have believed them. The clock stood, of course, in the corner, a moonbeam floated idly on the floor, and a little mauve mouse came from the hole in the chimney corner and frisked and scampered in the light of the moonbeam upon the floor. The little mauve mouse was particularly merry; sometimes she danced upon two legs and sometimes upon four legs, but always very daintily and always very merrily.

"Ah, me!" sighed the old clock, "how different mice are nowadays from the mice we used to have in the good old times! Now there was your grandma, Mistress Velvetpaw, and there was your grandpa, Master Sniffwhisker,—how grave and dignified they were! Many a night have I seen them dancing upon the carpet below me, but always the stately minuet and never that crazy frisking which you are executing now, to my surprise—yes, and to my horror, too."

"But why shouldn't I be merry?" asked the little mauve mouse. "To-morrow is Christmas, and this is Christmas eve."

"So it is," said the old clock. "I had really forgotten all about it. But tell me, what is Christmas to you, little Miss Mauve Mouse?"

"A great deal to me!" cried the little mauve mouse. "I have been very good a very long time: I have not used any bad words, nor have I gnawed any holes, nor have I stolen any canary seed, nor have I worried my mother by running behind the flour-barrel where that horrid trap is set. In fact, I have been so good that I'm very sure Santa Claus will bring me something very pretty."

This seemed to amuse the old clock mightily; in fact, the old clock fell to laughing so heartily that in an unguarded moment she struck twelve instead of ten, which was exceedingly careless and therefore to be reprehended.

"Why, you silly little mauve mouse," said the old clock, "you don't believe in Santa Claus, do you?"

"Of course I do," answered the little mauve mouse. "Believe in Santa Claus? Why shouldn't I? Didn't Santa Claus bring me a beautiful butter-cracker last Christmas, and a lovely gingersnap, and a delicious rind of cheese, and—and—lots of things? I should be very ungrateful if I did not believe in Santa Claus, and I certainly shall not disbelieve in him at the very moment when I am expecting him to arrive with a bundle of goodies for me.

"I once had a little sister," continued the little mauve mouse, "who did not believe in Santa Claus, and the very thought of the fate that befell her makes my blood run cold and my whiskers stand on end. She died before I was born, but my mother has told me all about her. Perhaps you never saw her; her name was Squeaknibble, and she was in stature one of those long, low, rangy mice that are seldom found in well-stocked pantries. Mother says that Squeaknibble took after our ancestors who came from New England, where the malignant ingenuity of the people and the ferocity of the cats rendered life precarious indeed. Squeaknibble seemed to inherit many ancestral traits, the most conspicuous of which was a disposition to sneer at some of the most respected dogmas in mousedom. From her very infancy she doubted, for example, the widely accepted theory that the moon was composed of green cheese; and this heresy was the first intimation her parents had of the sceptical turn of her mind. Of course, her parents were vastly annoyed, for their maturer natures saw that this youthful scepticism portended serious, if not fatal, consequences. Yet all in vain did the sagacious couple reason and plead with their headstrong and heretical child.

"For a long time Squeaknibble would not believe that there was any such archfiend as a cat; but she came to be convinced to the contrary one memorable night, on which occasion she lost two inches of her beautiful tail, and received so terrible a fright that for fully an hour afterward her little heart beat so violently as to lift her off her feet and bump her head against the top of our domestic hole. The cat that deprived my sister of so large a percentage of her vertebral colophon was the same brindled ogress that nowadays steals ever and anon into this room, crouches treacherously behind the sofa, and feigns to be asleep, hoping, forsooth, that some of us, heedless of her hated presence, will venture within reach of her diabolical claws. So enraged was this ferocious monster at the escape of my sister that she ground her fangs viciously together, and vowed to take no pleasure in life until she held in her devouring jaws the innocent little mouse which belonged to the mangled bit of tail she even then clutched in her remorseless claws."

"Yes," said the old clock, "now that you recall the incident, I recollect it well. I was here then, in this very corner, and I remember that I laughed at the cat and chided her for her awkwardness. My reproaches irritated her; she told me that a clock's duty was to run itself down, not to be depreciating the merits of others! Yes, I recall the time; that cat's tongue is fully as sharp as her claws."

"Be that as it may," said the little mauve mouse, "it is a matter of history, and therefore beyond dispute, that from that very moment the cat pined for Squeaknibble's life; it seemed as if that one little two-inch taste of Squeaknibble's tail had filled the cat with a consuming passion, or appetite, for the rest of Squeaknibble. So the cat waited and watched and hunted and schemed and devised and did everything possible for a cat—a cruel cat—to do in order to gain her murderous ends. One night—one fatal Christmas eve—our mother had undressed the children for bed, and was urging upon them to go to sleep earlier than usual, since she fully expected that Santa Claus would bring each of them something very palatable and nice before morning. Thereupon the little dears whisked their cunning tails, pricked up their beautiful ears, and began telling one another what they hoped Santa Claus would bring. One asked for a slice of Roquefort, another for Neufchatel, another for Sap Sago, and a fourth for Edam; one expressed a preference for de Brie, while another hoped to get

Parmesan; one clamored for imperial blue Stilton, and another craved the fragrant boon of Caprera. There were fourteen little ones then, and consequently there were diverse opinions as to the kind of gift which Santa Claus should best bring; still, there was, as you can readily understand, an enthusiastic unanimity upon this point, namely, that the gift should be cheese of some brand or other.

"'My dears,' said our mother, 'what matters it whether the boon which Santa Claus brings be royal English cheddar or fromage de Bricquebec, Vermont sage, or Herkimer County skim-milk? We should be content with whatsoever Santa Claus bestows, so long as it be cheese, disjoined from all traps whatsoever, unmixed with Paris green, and free from glass, strychnine, and other harmful ingredients. As for myself, I shall be satisfied with a cut of nice, fresh Western reserve; for truly I recognize in no other viand or edible half the fragrance or half the gustfulness to be met with in one of these pale but aromatic domestic products. So run away to your dreams now, that Santa Claus may find you sleeping.'

"The children obeyed,—all but Squeaknibble. 'Let the others think what they please,' said she, 'but I don't believe in Santa Claus. I'm not going to bed, either. I'm going to creep out of this dark hole and have a quiet romp, all by myself, in the moonlight.' Oh, what a vain, foolish, wicked little mouse was Squeaknibble! But I will not reproach the dead; her punishment came all too swiftly. Now listen: who do you suppose overheard her talking so disrespectfully of Santa Claus?"

"Why, Santa Claus himself," said the old clock.

"Oh, no," answered the little mauve mouse. "It was that wicked, murderous cat! Just as Satan lurks and lies in wait for bad children, so does the cruel cat lurk and lie in wait for naughty little mice. And you can depend upon it that, when that awful cat heard Squeaknibble speak so disrespectfully of Santa Claus, her wicked eyes glowed with joy, her sharp teeth watered, and her bristling fur emitted electric sparks as big as marrowfat peas. Then what did that blood-thirsty monster do but scuttle as fast as she could into Dear-my-Soul's room, leap up into Dear-my-Soul's crib, and walk off with the pretty little white muff which Dear-my-Soul used to wear when she went for a visit to the little girl in the next block! What upon earth did the horrid old cat want with Dear-my-Soul's pretty little white muff? Ah, the duplicity, the diabolical ingenuity of that cat! Listen.

"In the first place," resumed the little mauve mouse, after a pause that testified eloquently to the depth of her emotion,—"in the first place, that wretched cat dressed herself up in that pretty little white muff, by which you are to understand that she crawled through the muff just so far as to leave her four cruel legs at liberty."

"Yes, I understand," said the old clock.

"Then she put on the boy doll's fur cap," said the little mauve mouse, "and when she was arrayed in the boy doll's fur cap and Dear-my-Soul's pretty little white muff, of course she didn't look like a cruel cat at all. But whom did she look like?"

"Like the boy doll," suggested the old clock.

"No, no!" cried the little mauve mouse.

"Like Dear-my-Soul?" asked the old clock.

"How stupid you are!" exclaimed the little mauve mouse. "Why, she looked like Santa Claus, of course!"

"Oh, yes; I see," said the old clock. "Now I begin to be interested; go on."

"Alas!" sighed the little mauve mouse, "not much remains to be told; but there is more of my story left than there was of Squeaknibble when that horrid cat crawled out of that miserable disguise. You are to understand that, contrary to her sagacious mother's injunction, and in notorious derision of the mooted coming of Santa Claus, Squeaknibble issued from the friendly hole in the chimney corner, and gambolled about over this very carpet, and, I dare say, in this very moonlight."

"I do not know," said the moonbeam faintly. "I am so very old, and I have seen so many things—I do not know."

"Right merrily was Squeaknibble gambolling," continued the little mauve mouse, "and she had just turned a double back somersault without the use of what remained of her tail, when, all of a sudden, she beheld, looming up like a monster ghost, a figure all in white fur! Oh, how frightened she was, and how her little heart did beat! 'Purr, purr-r-r,' said the ghost in white fur. 'Oh, please don't hurt me!' pleaded Squeaknibble. 'No; I'll not hurt you,' said the ghost in white fur; 'I'm Santa Claus, and I've brought you a beautiful piece of savory old cheese, you dear little mousie, you.' Poor Squeaknibble was deceived; a sceptic all her life, she was at last befooled by the most palpable and most fatal of frauds. 'How good of you!' said Squeaknibble. 'I didn't believe there was a Santa Claus, and—' but before she could say more she was seized by two sharp, cruel claws that conveyed her crushed body to the murderous mouth of mousedom's most malignant foe. I can dwell no longer upon this harrowing scene. Suffice it to say that ere the morrow's sun rose like a big yellow Herkimer County cheese upon the spot where that tragedy had been enacted, poor Squeaknibble passed to that bourn whence two inches of her beautiful tail had preceded her by the space of three weeks to a day. As for Santa Claus, when he came that Christmas eve, bringing morceaux de Brie and of Stilton for the other little mice, he heard with sorrow of Squeaknibble's fate; and ere he departed he said that in all his experience he had never known of a mouse or of a child that had prospered after once saying that he didn't believe in Santa Claus."

"Well, that is a remarkable story," said the old clock. "But if you believe in Santa Claus, why aren't you in bed?"

"That's where I shall be presently," answered the little mauve mouse, "but I must have my scamper, you know. It is very pleasant, I assure you, to frolic in the light of the moon; only I cannot understand why you are always so cold and so solemn and so still, you pale, pretty little moonbeam."

"Indeed, I do not know that I am so," said the moonbeam. "But I am very old, and I have travelled many, many leagues, and I have seen wondrous things. Sometimes I toss upon the ocean, sometimes I fall upon a slumbering flower, sometimes I rest upon a dead child's face. I see the fairies at their play, and I hear mothers singing lullabies. Last night I swept across the frozen bosom of a river. A woman's face looked up at me; it was the picture of eternal rest. 'She is sleeping,' said the frozen river. 'I rock her to and fro, and sing to her. Pass gently by, O moonbeam; pass gently by, lest you awaken her.'"

"How strangely you talk," said the old clock. "Now, I'll warrant me that, if you wanted to, you could tell many a pretty and wonderful story. You must know many a Christmas tale; pray, tell us one to wear away this night of Christmas watching."

"I know but one," said the moonbeam. "I have told it over and over again, in every land and in every home; yet I do not weary of it. It is very simple. Should you like to hear it?"

"Indeed we should," said the old clock; "but before you begin, let me strike twelve; for I shouldn't want to interrupt you."

When the old clock had performed this duty with somewhat more than usual alacrity, the moonbeam began its story:

"Upon a time—so long ago that I can't tell how long ago it was—I fell upon a hill-side. It was in a far distant country; this I know, because, although it was the Christmas time, it was not in that country as it is wont to be in countries to the north. Hither the snow-king never came; flowers bloomed all the year, and at all times the lambs found pleasant pasturage on the hill-sides. The night wind was balmy, and there was a fragrance of cedar in its breath. There were violets on the hill-side, and I fell amongst them and lay there. I kissed them, and they awakened. 'Ah, is it you, little moonbeam?' they said, and they nestled in the grass which the lambs had left uncropped.

"A shepherd lay upon a broad stone on the hill-side; above him spread an olive-tree, old, ragged, and gloomy; but now it swayed its rusty branches majestically in the shifting air of night. The shepherd's name was Benoni. Wearied with long watching, he had fallen asleep; his crook had slipped from his hand. Upon the hill-side, too, slept the shepherd's flock. I had counted them again and again; I had stolen across their gentle faces and brought them pleasant dreams of green pastures and of cool water-brooks. I had kissed old Benoni, too, as he lay slumbering there; and in his dreams he seemed to see Israel's King come upon earth, and in his dreams he murmured the promised Messiah's name.

"'Ah, is it you, little moonbeam?' quoth the violets. 'You have come in good time. Nestle here with us, and see wonderful things come to pass.'

"'What are these wonderful things of which you speak?' I asked.

"'We heard the old olive-tree telling of them to-night,' said the violets. 'Do not go to sleep, little violets,' said the old olive-tree, 'for this is Christmas night, and the Master shall walk upon the hill-side in the glory of the midnight hour.' So we waited and watched; one by one the lambs fell asleep; one by one the stars peeped out; the shepherd nodded and crooned, and crooned and nodded, and at last he, too, went fast asleep, and his crook slipped from his keeping. Then we called to the old olive-tree yonder, asking how soon the midnight hour would come; but all the old olive-tree answered was 'Presently, presently,' and finally we, too, fell asleep, wearied by our long watching, and lulled by the rocking and swaying of the old olive-tree in the breezes of the night.

"'But who is this Master?' I asked.

"'A child, a little child,' they answered. 'He is called the little Master by the others. He comes here often, and plays among the flowers of the hill-side. Sometimes the lambs, gambolling too carelessly, have crushed and bruised us so that we lie bleeding and are like to die; but the little Master heals our wounds and refreshes us once again.'

"I marvelled much to hear these things. 'The midnight hour is at hand,' said I, 'and I will abide with you to see this little Master of whom you speak.' So we nestled among the verdure of the hill-side, and sang songs one to another.

"'Come away!' called the night wind; 'I know a beauteous sea not far hence, upon whose bosom you shall float, float, float away out into the mists and clouds, if you will come with me.'

"But I hid under the violets and amid the tall grass, that the night wind might not woo me with its pleading. 'Ho, there, old olive-tree!' cried the violets; 'do you see the little Master coming? Is not the midnight hour at hand?'

"'I can see the town yonder,' said the old olive-tree. 'A star beams bright over Bethlehem, the iron gates swing open, and the little Master comes.'

"Two children came to the hill-side. The one, older than his comrade, was Dimas, the son of Benoni. He was rugged and sinewy, and over his brown shoulders was flung a goatskin; a leathern cap did not confine his long, dark curly hair. The other child was he whom they called the little Master; about his slender form clung raiment white as snow, and around his face of heavenly innocence fell curls of golden yellow. So beautiful a child I had not seen before, nor have I ever since seen such as he. And as they came together to the hill-side, there seemed to glow about the little Master's head a soft white light, as if the moon had sent its tenderest, fairest beams to kiss those golden curls.

"'What sound was that?' cried Dimas, for he was exceeding fearful.

"'Have no fear, Dimas,' said the little Master. 'Give me thy hand, and I will lead thee.'

"Presently they came to the rock whereon Benoni, the shepherd, lay; and they stood under the old olive-tree, and the old olive-tree swayed no longer in the night wind, but bent its branches reverently in the presence of the little Master. It seemed as if the wind, too, stayed in its shifting course just then; for suddenly there was a solemn hush, and you could hear no noise, except that in his dreams Benoni spoke the Messiah's name.

"'Thy father sleeps,' said the little Master, 'and it is well that it is so; for that I love thee Dimas, and that thou shalt walk with me in my Father's kingdom, I would show thee the glories of my birthright.'

"Then all at once sweet music filled the air, and light, greater than the light of day, illumined the sky and fell upon all that hill-side. The heavens opened, and angels, singing joyous songs, walked to the earth. More wondrous still, the stars, falling from their places in the sky, clustered upon the old olive-tree, and swung hither and thither like colored lanterns. The flowers of the hill-side all awakened, and they, too, danced and sang. The angels, coming hither, hung gold and silver and jewels and precious stones upon the old olive, where swung the stars; so that the glory of that sight, though I might live forever, I shall never see again. When Dimas heard and saw these things he fell upon his knees, and catching the hem of the little Master's garment, he kissed it.

"'Greater joy than this shall be thine, Dimas,' said the little Master; 'but first must all things be fulfilled.'

"All through that Christmas night did the angels come and go with their sweet anthems; all through that Christmas night did the stars dance and sing; and when it came my time to steal away, the hill-side was still beautiful with the glory and the music of heaven."

"Well, is that all?" asked the old clock.

"No," said the moonbeam; "but I am nearly done. The years went on. Sometimes I tossed upon the ocean's bosom, sometimes I scampered o'er a battle-field, sometimes I lay upon a dead child's face. I heard the voices of Darkness and mothers' lullabies and sick men's prayers—and so the years went on.

"I fell one night upon a hard and furrowed face. It was of ghostly pallor. A thief was dying on the cross, and this was his wretched face. About the cross stood men with staves and swords and spears, but none paid heed unto the thief. Somewhat beyond this cross another was lifted up, and upon it was stretched a human body my light fell not upon. But I heard a voice that somewhere I had heard before,—though where I did not know,—and this voice blessed those that railed and jeered and shamefully entreated. And suddenly the voice called 'Dimas, Dimas!' and the thief upon whose hardened face I rested made answer.

"Then I saw that it was Dimas; yet to this wicked criminal there remained but little of the shepherd child whom I had seen in all his innocence upon the hill-side. Long years of sinful life had seared their marks into his face; yet now, at the sound of that familiar voice, somewhat of the old-time boyish look came back, and in the yearning of the anguished eyes I seemed to see the shepherd's son again.

"'The Master!' cried Dimas, and he stretched forth his neck that he might see him that spake.

"'O Dimas, how art thou changed!' cried the Master, yet there was in his voice no tone of rebuke save that which cometh of love.

"Then Dimas wept, and in that hour he forgot his pain. And the Master's consoling voice and the Master's presence there wrought in the dying criminal such a new spirit, that when at last his head fell upon his bosom, and the men about the cross said that he was dead, it seemed as if I shined not upon a felon's face, but upon the face of the gentle shepherd lad, the son of Benoni.

"And shining on that dead and peaceful face, I bethought me of the little Master's words that he had spoken under the old olive-tree upon the hill-side: 'Your eyes behold the promised glory now, O Dimas,' I whispered, 'for with the Master you walk in Paradise.'"

Ah, little Dear-my-Soul, you know—you know whereof the moonbeam spake. The shepherd's bones are dust, the flocks are scattered, the old olive-tree is gone, the flowers of the hill-side are withered, and none knoweth where the grave of Dimas is made. But last night, again, there shined a star over Bethlehem, and the angels descended from the sky to earth, and the stars sang together in glory. And the bells,—hear them, little Dear-my-Soul, how sweetly they are ringing,—the bells bear us the good tidings of great joy this Christmas morning, that our Christ is born, and that with him he bringeth peace on earth and good-will toward men.

CHRISTMAS MORNING

The angel host that sped last night,
Bearing the wondrous news afar,
Came in their ever-glorious flight
Unto a slumbering little star.

"Awake and sing, O star!" they cried.
"Awake and glorify the morn!
Herald the tidings far and wide—
He that shall lead His flock is born!"

The little star awoke and sung
As only stars in rapture may,
And presently where church bells hung
The joyous tidings found their way.

"Awake, O bells! 't is Christmas morn—
Awake and let thy music tell
To all mankind that now is born
What Shepherd loves His lambkins well!"

Then rang the bells as fled the night
O'er dreaming land and drowsing deep,
And coming with the morning light,
They called, my child, to you asleep.

Sweetly and tenderly they spoke,
And lingering round your little bed,
Their music pleaded till you woke,
And this is what their music said:

"Awake and sing! 'tis Christmas morn,
Whereon all earth salutes her King!
In Bethlehem is the Shepherd born.
Awake, O little lamb, and sing!"

So, dear my child, kneel at my feet,
And with those voices from above
Share thou this holy time with me,
The universal hymn of love.

December 25, 1890.

MISTRESS MERCILESS

This is to tell of our little Mistress Merciless, who for a season abided with us, but is now and forever gone from us unto the far-off land of Ever-Plaisance. The tale is soon told; for it were not seemly to speak all the things that are in one's heart when one hath to say of a much-beloved child, whose life here hath been shortened so that, in God's wisdom and kindness, her life shall be longer in that garden that bloometh far away.

You shall know that all did call her Mistress Merciless; but her mercilessness was of a sweet, persuasive kind: for with the beauty of her face and the music of her voice and the exceeding sweetness of her virtues was she wont to slay all hearts; and this she did unwittingly, for she was a little child. And so it was in love that we did call her Mistress Merciless, just as it was in love that she did lord it over all our hearts.

Upon a time walked she in a full fair garden, and there went with her an handmaiden that we did call in merry wise the Queen of Sheba; for this handmaiden was in sooth no queen at all, but a sorry and ill-favored wench; but she was assotted upon our little Mistress Merciless and served her diligently, and for that good reason was vastly beholden of us all. Yet, in a jest, we called her the Queen of Sheba; and I make a venture that she looked exceeding fair in the eyes of our little Mistress Merciless: for the eyes of children look not upon the faces but into the hearts and souls of others. Whilst these two walked in the full fair garden at that time they came presently unto an arbor wherein there was a rustic seat, which was called the Siege of Restfulness; and hereupon sate a little sick boy that, from his birth, had been lame, so that he could not play and make merry with other children, but was wont to come every day into this full fair garden and content himself with the companionship of the flowers. And, though he was a little lame boy, he never trod upon those flowers; and even had he done so, methinks the pressure of those crippled feet had been a caress, for the little lame boy was filled with the spirit of love and tenderness. As the tiniest, whitest, shrinking flower exhaleth the most precious perfume, so in and from this little lame boy's life there came a grace that was hallowing in its beauty.

Since they never before had seen him, they asked him his name; and he answered them that of those at home he was called Master Sweetheart, a name he could not understand: for surely, being a cripple, he must be a very sorry sweetheart; yet, that he was a sweetheart unto his mother at least he had no doubt, for she did love to hold him in her lap and call him by that name; and many times when she did so he saw that tears were in her eyes,—a proof, she told him when he asked, that Master Sweetheart was her sweetheart before all others upon earth.

It befell that our little Mistress Merciless and Master Sweetheart became fast friends, and the Queen of Sheba was handmaiden to them both; for the simple, loyal creature had not a mind above the artless prattle of childhood, and the strange allegory of the lame boy's speech filled her with awe, even as the innocent lisping of our little Mistress Merciless delighted her heart and came within the comprehension of her limited understanding. So each day, when it was fair, these three came into the full fair garden, and rambled there together; and when they were weary they entered into the arbor and sate together upon the Siege of Restfulness. Wit ye well there was not a flower or a tree or a shrub or a bird in all that full fair garden which they did not know and love, and in very sooth every flower and tree and shrub and bird therein did know and love them.

When they entered into the arbor, and sate together upon the Siege of Restfulness, it was Master Sweetheart's wont to tell them of the land of Ever-Plaisance, for it was a conceit of his that he journeyed each day nearer and nearer to that land, and that his journey thitherward was nearly done. How came he to know of that land I cannot say, for I do not know; but I am fain to believe that, as he said, the exceeding fair angels told him thereof when by night, as he lay sleeping, they came singing and with caresses to his bedside.

I speak now of a holy thing, therefore I speak truth when I say that while little children lie sleeping in their beds at night it pleaseth God to send His exceeding fair angels with singing and caresses to bear messages of His love unto those little sleeping children. And I have seen those exceeding fair angels bend with folded wings over the little cradles and the little beds, and kiss those little sleeping children and whisper God's messages of love to them, and I knew that those messages were full of sweet tidings; for, even though they slept, the little children smiled. This have I seen, and there is none who loveth little children that will deny the truth of this thing which I have now solemnly declared.

Of that land of Ever-Plaisance was our little Mistress Merciless ever fain to hear tell. But when she beset the rest of us to speak thereof we knew not what to say other than to confirm such reports as Master Sweetheart had already made. For when it cometh to knowing of that far-off land,—ah me, who knoweth more than the veriest little child? And oftentimes within the bosom of a little, helpless, fading one there bloometh a wisdom which sages cannot comprehend. So when she asked us we were wont to bid her go to Master Sweetheart, for he knew the truth and spake it.

It is now to tell of an adventure which on a time befell in that full fair garden of which you have heard me speak. In this garden lived many birds of surpassing beauty and most rapturous song, and among them was one that they called Joyous, for that he did ever carol forth so joyously, it mattered not what the day soever might be. This bird Joyous had his home in the top of an exceeding high tree, hard by the pleasant arbor, and here did he use to sit at such times as the little people came into that arbor, and then would he sing to them such songs as befitted that quiet spot, and them that came thereto. But there was a full evil cat that dwelt near by, and this cruel beast found no pleasure in the music that Joyous did make continually; nay, that music filled this full evil cat with a wicked thirst for the blood of that singing innocent, and she had no peace for the malice that was within her seeking to devise a means whereby she might comprehend the bird Joyous to her murderous intent. Now you must know that it was the wont of our little Mistress Merciless and of Master Sweetheart to feed the birds in that fair garden with such crumbs as they were suffered to bring with them into the arbor, and at such times would those birds fly down with grateful twitterings and eat of those crumbs upon the greensward round about the arbor. Wit ye well, it was a merry sight to see those twittering birds making feast upon the good things which those children brought, and our little Mistress Merciless and little Master Sweetheart had sweet satisfaction therein. But, on a day, whilst thus those twittering birds made great feasting, lo! on a sudden did that full evil cat whereof I have spoken steal softly from a thicket, and with one hideous bound make her way into the very midst of those birds and seize upon that bird Joyous, that was wont to sing so merrily from the tree hard by the arbor. Oh, there was a mighty din and a fearful fluttering, and the rest flew swiftly away, but Joyous could not do so, because the full evil cat held him in her cruel fangs and claws. And I make no doubt that Joyous would speedily have met his death, but that with a wrathful cry did our little Mistress Merciless hasten to his rescue. And our little Mistress belabored that full evil cat with Master Sweetheart's crutch, until that cruel beast let loose her hold upon the fluttering bird and was full glad to escape with her aching bones into the thicket again. So it was that Joyous was recovered from death; but even then might it have fared ill with him, had they not taken him up and dressed his wounds and cared for him until duly he was well again. And then they released him to do his plaisance, and he returned to his home in the tree hard by the arbor and there he sung unto those children more sweetly than ever before; for his heart was full of gratitude to our little Mistress Merciless and Master Sweetheart.

Now, of the dolls that she had in goodly number, that one which was named Beautiful did our little Mistress Merciless love best. Know well that the doll Beautiful had come not from oversea, and was neither of wax nor of china; but she was right ingeniously constructed of a bed-key that was made of wood, and unto the top of this bed-key had the Queen of Sheba superadded a head with a fair face, and upon the body and the arms of the key had she hung passing noble raiment. Unto this doll Beautiful was our little Mistress Merciless vastly beholden, and she did use to have the doll Beautiful lie by her side at night whilst she slept, and whithersoever during the day she went, there also would she take the doll Beautiful, too. Much sorrow and lamentation, therefore, made our little Mistress Merciless when on an evil day the doll Beautiful by chance fell into the fish-pond, and was not rescued therefrom until one of her beauteous eyes had been devoured of the envious water; so that ever thereafter the doll Beautiful had but one eye, and that, forsooth, was grievously faded. And on another evil day came a monster ribald dog pup and seized upon the doll Beautiful whilst she reposed in the arbor, and bore her away, and romped boisterously with her upon the sward, and tore off her black-thread hair, and sought to destroy her wholly, which surely he would have done but for the Queen of Sheba, who made haste to rescue the doll Beautiful, and chastise that monster ribald dog pup.

Therefore, as you can understand, the time was right busily spent. The full fair garden, with its flowers and the singing birds and the gracious arbor and the Siege of Restfulness, found favor with those children, and amid these joyous scenes did Master Sweetheart have to tell each day of that far-off land of Ever-Plaisance, whither he said he was going. And one day, when the sun shone very bright, and the full fair garden joyed in the music of those birds, Master Sweetheart did not come, and they missed the little lame boy and wondered where he was. And as he never came again they thought at last that of a surety he had departed into that country whereof he loved to tell. Which thing filled our little Mistress Merciless with wonder and inquiry; and I think she was lonely ever after that,—lonely for Master Sweetheart.

I am thinking now of her and of him; for this is the Christmas season,—the time when it is most meet to think of the children and other sweet and holy things. There is snow everywhere, snow and cold. The garden is desolate and voiceless: the flowers are gone, the trees are ghosts, the birds have departed. It is winter out there, and it is winter, too, in this heart of mine. Yet in this Christmas season I think of them, and it pleaseth me—God forbid that I offend with much speaking—it pleaseth me to tell of the little things they did and loved. And you shall understand it all if, perchance, this sacred Christmas time a little Mistress Merciless of your own, or a little Master Sweetheart, clingeth to your knee and sanctifieth your hearth-stone.

When of an evening all the joy of day was done, would our little Mistress Merciless fall aweary; and then her eyelids would grow exceeding heavy and her little tired hands were fain to fold. At such a time it was my wont to beguile her weariness with little tales of faery, or with the gentle play that sleepy children like. Much was her fancy taken with what I told her of the train that every night whirleth away to Shut-Eye Town, bearing unto that beauteous country sleepy little girls and boys. Nor would she be content until I told her thereof,—yes, every night whilst I robed her in her cap and gown would she demand of me that tale of Shut-Eye Town, and the wonderful train that was to bear her thither. Then would I say in this wise:

At Bedtime-ville there is a train of cars that waiteth for you, my sweet,—for you and for other little ones that would go to quiet, slumbrous Shut-Eye Town.

But make no haste; there is room for all. Each hath a tiny car that is snug and warm, and when the train starteth each car swingeth soothingly this way and that way, this way and that way, through all the journey of the night.

Your little gown is white and soft; your little cap will hold those pretty curls so fast that they cannot get away. Here is a curl that peepeth out to see what is going to happen. Hush, little curl! make no noise; we will let you peep out at the wonderful sights, but you must not tell the others about it; let them sleep, snuggled close together.

The locomotive is ready to start. Can you not hear it?

"Shug-chug! Shug-chug! Shug-chug!" That is what the locomotive is saying, all to itself. It knoweth how pleasant a journey it is about to make.

"Shug-chug! Shug-chug! Shug-chug!"

Oh, many a time hath it proudly swept over prairie and hill, over river and plain, through sleeping gardens and drowsy cities, swiftly and quietly, bearing the little ones to the far, pleasant valley where lieth Shut-Eye Town.

"Shug-chug! Shug-chug! Shug-chug!"

So sayeth the locomotive to itself at the station in Bedtime-ville; for it knoweth how fair and far a journey is before it.

Then a bell soundeth. Surely my little one heareth the bell!

"Ting-long! Ting-a-long! Ting-long!"

So soundeth the bell, and it seemeth to invite you to sleep and dreams.

"Ting-long! Ting-a-long! Ting-long!"

How sweetly ringeth and calleth that bell.

"To sleep—to dreams, O little lambs!" it seemeth to call. "Nestle down close, fold your hands, and shut your dear eyes! We are off and away to Shut-Eye Town! Ting-long! Ting-a-long! Ting-long! To sleep—to dreams, O little cosset lambs!"

And now the conductor calleth out in turn. "All aboard!" he calleth. "All aboard for Shut-Eye Town!" he calleth in a kindly tone.

But, hark ye, dear-my-soul, make thou no haste; there is room for all. Here is a cosey little car for you. How like your cradle it is, for it is snug and warm, and it rocketh this way and that way, this way and that way, all night long, and its pillows caress you tenderly. So step into the pretty nest, and in it speed to Shut-Eye Town.

"Toot! Toot!"

That is the whistle. It soundeth twice, but it must sound again before the train can start. Now you have nestled down, and your dear hands are folded; let your two eyes be folded, too, my sweet; for in a moment you shall be rocked away, and away, away into the golden mists of Balow!

"Ting-long! Ting-a-long! Ting-long!"

"All aboard!"

"Toot! Toot! Toot!"

And so my little golden apple is off and away for Shut-Eye Town!

Slowly moveth the train, yet faster by degrees. Your hands are folded, my beloved, and your dear eyes they are closed; and yet you see the beauteous sights that skirt the journey through the mists of Balow. And it is rockaway, rockaway, rockaway, that your speeding cradle goes,—rockaway, rockaway, rockaway, through the golden glories that lie in the path that leadeth to Shut-Eye Town.

"Toot! Toot!"

So crieth the whistle, and it is "down-brakes," for here we are at Ginkville, and every little one knoweth that pleasant waking-place, where mother with her gentle hands holdeth the gracious cup to her sleepy darling's lips.

"Ting-long! Ting-a-long! Ting-long!" and off is the train again. And swifter and swifter it speedeth,—oh, I am sure no other train speedeth half so swiftly! The sights my dear one sees! I cannot tell of them—one must see those beauteous sights to know how wonderful they are!

"Shug-chug! Shug-chug! Shug-chug!"

On and on and on the locomotive proudly whirleth the train.

"Ting-long! Ting-a-long! Ting-long!"

The bell calleth anon, but fainter and evermore fainter; and fainter and fainter groweth that other calling—"Toot! Toot! Toot!"—till finally I know that in that Shut-Eye Town afar my dear one dreameth the dreams of Balow.

This was the bedtime tale which I was wont to tell our little Mistress Merciless, and at its end I looked upon her face to see it calm and beautiful in sleep.

Then was I wont to kneel beside her little bed and fold my two hands,—thus,—and let my heart call to the host invisible: "O guardian angels of this little child, hold her in thy keeping from all the perils of darkness and the night! O sovereign Shepherd, cherish Thy little lamb and mine, and, Holy Mother, fold her to thy bosom and thy love! But give her back to me,—when morning cometh, restore ye unto me my little one!"

But once she came not back. She had spoken much of Master Sweetheart and of that land of Ever-Plaisance whither he had gone. And she was not afeard to make the journey alone; so once upon a time when our little Mistress Merciless bade us good-by, and went away forever, we knew that it were better so; for she was lonely here, and without her that far-distant country whither she journeyed were not content. Though our hearts were like to break for love of her, we knew that it were better so.

The tale is told, for it were not seemly to speak all the things that are in one's heart when one hath to say of a much-beloved child whose life here hath been shortened so that, in God's wisdom and kindness, her life shall be longer in that garden that bloometh far away.

About me are scattered the toys she loved, and the doll Beautiful hath come down all-battered and grim,—yet, oh! so very precious to me, from those distant years; yonder fareth the Queen of Sheba in her service as handmaiden unto me and mine,—gaunt and doleful-eyed, yet stanch and sturdy as of old. The garden lieth under the Christmas snow,—the garden where ghosts of trees wave their arms and moan over the graves of flowers; the once gracious arbor is crippled now with the infirmities of age, the Siege of Restfulness fast sinketh into decay, and long, oh! long ago did that bird Joyous carol forth his last sweet song in the garden that was once so passing fair.

And amid it all,—this heartache and the loneliness which the years have brought,—cometh my Christmas gift to-day: the solace of a vision of that country whither she—our little Mistress Merciless—hath gone; a glimpse of that far-off land of Ever-Plaisance.

BETHLEHEM-TOWN

As I was going to Bethlehem-town,
Upon the earth I cast me down
All underneath a little tree
That whispered in this wise to me:
"Oh, I shall stand on Calvary
And bear what burthen saveth thee!"

As up I fared to Bethlehem-town,
I met a shepherd coming down,
And thus he quoth: "A wondrous sight
Hath spread before mine eyes this night,—
An angel host most fair to see,
That sung full sweetly of a tree
That shall uplift on Calvary
What burthen saveth you and me!"

And as I gat to Bethlehem-town,
Lo! wise men came that bore a crown.
"Is there," cried I, "in Bethlehem
A King shall wear this diadem?"
"Good sooth," they quoth, "and it is He
That shall be lifted on the tree
And freely shed on Calvary
What blood redeemeth us and thee!"

Unto a Child in Bethlehem-town
The wise men came and brought the crown;
And while the infant smiling slept,
Upon their knees they fell and wept;
But, with her babe upon her knee,
Naught recked that Mother of the tree,
That should uplift on Calvary
What burthen saveth all and me.

Again I walk in Bethlehem-town
And think on Him that wears the crown.
I may not kiss His feet again,
Nor worship Him as did I then;
My King hath died upon the tree,
And hath outpoured on Calvary
What blood redeemeth you and me!

THE FIRST CHRISTMAS TREE

Once upon a time the forest was in a great commotion. Early in the evening the wise old cedars had shaken their heads ominously and predicted strange things. They had lived in the forest many, many years; but never had they seen such marvellous sights as were to be seen now in the sky, and upon the hills, and in the distant village.

"Pray tell us what you see," pleaded a little vine; "we who are not as tall as you can behold none of these wonderful things. Describe them to us, that we may enjoy them with you."

"I am filled with such amazement," said one of the cedars, "that I can hardly speak. The whole sky seems to be aflame, and the stars appear to be dancing among the clouds; angels walk down from heaven to the earth, and enter the village or talk with the shepherds upon the hills."

The vine listened in mute astonishment. Such things never before had happened. The vine trembled with excitement. Its nearest neighbor was a tiny tree, so small it scarcely ever was noticed; yet it was a very beautiful little tree, and the vines and ferns and mosses and other humble residents of the forest loved it dearly.

"How I should like to see the angels!" sighed the little tree, "and how I should like to see the stars dancing among the clouds! It must be very beautiful."

As the vine and the little tree talked of these things, the cedars watched with increasing interest the wonderful scenes over and beyond the confines of the forest. Presently they thought they heard music, and they were not mistaken, for soon the whole air was full of the sweetest harmonies ever heard upon earth.

"What beautiful music!" cried the little tree. "I wonder whence it comes."

"The angels are singing," said a cedar; "for none but angels could make such sweet music."

"But the stars are singing, too," said another cedar; "yes, and the shepherds on the hills join in the song, and what a strangely glorious song it is!"

The trees listened to the singing, but they did not understand its meaning: it seemed to be an anthem, and it was of a Child that had been born; but further than this they did not understand. The strange and glorious song continued all the night; and all that night the angels walked to and fro, and the shepherd-folk talked with the angels, and the stars danced and carolled in high heaven. And it was nearly morning when the cedars cried out, "They are coming to the forest! the angels are coming to the forest!" And, surely enough, this was true. The vine and the little tree were very terrified, and they begged their older and stronger neighbors to protect them from harm. But the cedars were too busy with their own fears to pay any heed to the faint pleadings of the humble vine and the little tree. The angels came into the forest, singing the same glorious anthem about the Child, and the stars sang in chorus with them, until every part of the woods rang with echoes of that wondrous song. There was nothing in the appearance of this angel host to inspire fear; they were clad all in white, and there were crowns upon their fair heads, and golden harps in their hands; love, hope, charity, compassion, and joy beamed from their beautiful faces, and their presence seemed to fill the forest with a divine peace. The angels came through the forest to where the little tree stood, and gathering around it, they touched it with their hands, and kissed its little branches, and sang even more sweetly than before. And their song was about the Child, the Child, the Child that had been born. Then the stars came down from the skies and danced and hung upon the branches of the tree, and they, too, sang that song,—the song of the Child. And all the other trees and the vines and the ferns and the mosses beheld in wonder; nor could they understand why all these things were being done, and why this exceeding honor should be shown the little tree.

When the morning came the angels left the forest,—all but one angel, who remained behind and lingered near the little tree. Then a cedar asked: "Why do you tarry with us, holy angel?" And the angel answered: "I stay to guard this little tree, for it is sacred, and no harm shall come to it."

The little tree felt quite relieved by this assurance, and it held up its head more confidently than ever before. And how it thrived and grew, and waxed in strength and beauty! The cedars said they never had seen the like. The sun seemed to lavish its choicest rays upon the little tree, heaven dropped its sweetest dew upon it, and the winds never came to the forest that they did not forget their rude manners and linger to kiss the little tree and sing it their prettiest songs. No danger ever menaced it, no harm threatened; for the angel never slept,—through the day and through the night the angel watched the little tree and protected it from all evil. Oftentimes the trees talked with the angel; but of course they understood little of what he said, for he spoke always of the Child who was to become the Master; and always when thus he talked, he caressed the little tree, and stroked its branches and leaves, and moistened them with his tears. It all was so very strange that none in the forest could understand.

So the years passed, the angel watching his blooming charge. Sometimes the beasts strayed toward the little tree and threatened to devour its tender foliage; sometimes the woodman came with his axe, intent upon hewing down the straight and comely thing; sometimes the hot, consuming breath of drought swept from the south, and sought to blight the forest and all its verdure: the angel kept them from the little tree. Serene and beautiful it grew, until now it was no longer a little tree, but the pride and glory of the forest.

One day the tree heard some one coming through the forest. Hitherto the angel had hastened to its side when men approached; but now the angel strode away and stood under the cedars yonder.

"Dear angel," cried the tree, "can you not hear the footsteps of some one approaching? Why do you leave me?"

"Have no fear," said the angel; "for He who comes is the Master."

The Master came to the tree and beheld it. He placed His hands upon its smooth trunk and branches, and the tree was thrilled with a strange and glorious delight. Then He stooped and kissed the tree, and then He turned and went away.

Many times after that the Master came to the forest, and when He came it always was to where the tree stood. Many times He rested beneath the tree and enjoyed the shade of its foliage, and listened to the music of the wind as it swept through the rustling leaves. Many times He slept there, and the tree watched over Him, and the forest was still, and all its voices were hushed. And the angel hovered near like a faithful sentinel.

Ever and anon men came with the Master to the forest, and sat with Him in the shade of the tree, and talked with Him of matters which the tree never could understand; only it heard that the talk was of love and charity and gentleness, and it saw that the Master was beloved and venerated by the others. It heard them tell of the Master's goodness and humility,—how He had healed the sick and raised the dead and bestowed inestimable blessings wherever He walked. And the tree loved the Master for His beauty and His goodness; and when He came to the forest it was full of joy, but when He came not it was sad. And the other trees of the forest joined in its happiness and its sorrow, for they, too, loved the Master. And the angel always hovered near.

The Master came one night alone into the forest, and His face was pale with anguish and wet with tears, and He fell upon His knees and prayed. The tree heard Him, and all the forest was still, as if it were standing in the presence of death. And when the morning came, lo! the angel had gone.

Then there was a great confusion in the forest. There was a sound of rude voices, and a clashing of swords and staves. Strange men appeared, uttering loud oaths and cruel threats, and the tree was filled with terror. It called aloud for the angel, but the angel came not.

"Alas," cried the vine, "they have come to destroy the tree, the pride and glory of the forest!"

The forest was sorely agitated, but it was in vain. The strange men plied their axes with cruel vigor, and the tree was hewn to the ground. Its beautiful branches were cut away and cast aside, and its soft, thick foliage was strewn to the tenderer mercies of the winds.

"They are killing me!" cried the tree; "why is not the angel here to protect me?"

But no one heard the piteous cry,—none but the other trees of the forest; and they wept, and the little vine wept too.

Then the cruel men dragged the despoiled and hewn tree from the forest, and the forest saw that beauteous thing no more.

But the night wind that swept down from the City of the Great King that night to ruffle the bosom of distant Galilee, tarried in the forest awhile to say that it had seen that day a cross upraised on Calvary,—the tree on which was stretched the body of the dying Master.

STAR OF THE EAST

Star of the East, that long ago
Brought wise men on their way
Where, angels singing to and fro,
The Child of Bethlehem lay—
Above that Syrian hill afar
Thou shinest out to-night, O Star!

Star of the East, the night were drear
But for the tender grace
That with thy glory comes to cheer
Earth's loneliest, darkest place;
For by that charity we see
Where there is hope for all and me.

Star of the East! show us the way
In wisdom undefiled
To seek that manger out and lay
Our gifts before the child—
To bring our hearts and offer them
Unto our King in Bethlehem!

Eugene Field was born on 2nd September, 1850 in St. Louis, Missouri at 634 S. Broadway to parents Roswell Martin and Frances Reed Field, both of New England stock. Tragically Field lost his mother at age 6 and was thereafter brought up by a cousin, Mary Field French, in Amherst, Massachusetts.

Field attended Williams College in Williamstown, Massachusetts.

When he was 19 his father died, and Field dropped out of Williams. Field's father, Roswell Martin Field, was the lawyer for Dred Scott, the slave who famously sued for his freedom. The complaint was sometimes referred to as 'The lawsuit that started the Civil War'.

Field then went to Knox College in Galesburg, Illinois, but again dropped out. This time after a year. However he did then summon himself to attend the University of Missouri in Columbia, Missouri, where his brother Roswell was studying. As can be gathered from his efforts to date Field was not the most serious of students but was gaining the reputation of being a prankster. Among his more outlandish attempts were a raid on the president's wine cellar, painting the president's house in school colors, and firing the school's landmark cannons at midnight.

Field tried acting but found it not to his liking, studied law but with little success, but did have an interest in writing for the student newspaper.

When his studies finished in 1871, although he never graduated, he collected his share of his inheritance from his father's estate, and set off for a trip to explore Europe. After six months, with funds from the inheritance exhausted, he returned to the United States.

Field then set to work as a journalist for the St. Joseph Gazette in Saint Joseph, Missouri, in 1875.

That same year he married the sixteen-year-old Julia Sutherland Comstock of St Joseph, Missouri. They would eventually have eight children during their twenty-two years of marriage, of whom only five would reach adulthood. Field, knowing that his understanding of finances was somewhat poor, arranged for all the money he earned to be sent to his wife for her to administer on behalf of the family.

In his career as a journalist he soon found a niche that suited him. His articles were light, humorous and written in a personal and gossipy style that endeared him to his readership. Some were soon being syndicated to other newspapers around the States. Field rose to be the city editor of the Gazette.

From 1876 through 1880, the Family lived in St. Louis. Field worked initially as an editorial writer for the Morning Journal and then for the Times-Journal. From there he worked for a short time as the managing editor of the Kansas City Times before settling, for two years, as the editor of the Denver Tribune. He also wrote a column for the paper, 'Odds and Ends,' poking fun at the climate, the muddy roads, the frontier language, and other aspects of Denver life. However his readership was large and growing. Further opportunities would come.

In 1883 the Field moved the family to Chicago lured by a salary of $50 a week. Field now began work for the Chicago Daily News. Here he wrote his humorous newspaper column called Sharps and Flats. He quickly found out that $50 dollars in Denver didn't stretch that far in bustling Chicago.

His column ran in the newspaper's morning edition. In it Field made quips about issues and personalities of the day, especially regarding the arts and literature. His pet subject was the intellectual superiority of Chicago, especially when he compared it to Boston, which he often did. In

April 1887, he wrote, "While Chicago is humping herself in the interests of literature, art and the sciences, vain old Boston is frivoling away her precious time in an attempted renaissance of the cod fisheries."

In another article that year after Chicago's National League baseball club sold future baseball Hall of Famer Mike "King" Kelly to Boston which overlapped with a speaking tour visit from the famous Boston poet and diplomat James Russell Lowell he wrote: "Chicago feels a special interest in Mr. Lowell at this particular time because he is perhaps the foremost representative of the enterprising and opulent community which within the last week has secured the services of one of Chicago's honored sons for the base-ball season of 1887. The fact that Boston has come to Chicago for the captain of her baseball nine has reinvigorated the bonds of affection between the metropolis of the Bay state and the metropolis of the mighty west; the truth of this will appear in the mighty welcome which our public will give Mr. Lowell next Tuesday."

It was in 1888 that his poem 'Little Boy Blue' was printed in America, a weekly journal. It achieved for Field instant and lasting fame. Coincidentally the same issue carried a poem by James Russell Lowell. Field was immensely pleased that his own poem was regarded with considerably more weight and acclaim.

Field had first published poetry in 1879, when his poem 'Christmas Treasures' was published. It later appeared in 'A Little Book of Western Verse' (1889). This was the beginning that would eventually number over a dozen volumes. He developed a style of light-hearted poems for children. Among the perennial favorites are 'Wynken, Blynken, and Nod' and 'The Duel' (but better known as 'The Gingham Dog and the Calico Cat') and 'Little Boy Blue' about the death of a child. As well as verse Field published an extensive range of short stories including 'The Holy Cross' and 'Daniel and the Devil.'

Field treasured rare, unusual and beautiful books and his personal library had scores of them. He also enjoyed making them too and frequently worked long hours with great care and various colored inks decorating the first letter of his poems.

In 1889 whilst the family were in London and Field himself was recovering from a bout of ill health he wrote his most famous poem; 'Lovers Lane'. It is often thought to have been written whilst the couple were courting but recent research settles it authorship to this later date. The poem was written as a reminder of better days when the couple courted in her father's buggy on 'Lover's Lane, St Jo'.

Field was ever curious and keen to push his boundaries. In 1891 with his brother Roswell they wrote and published 'Echoes from the Sabine Farm' a loosely translated version of Horace.

On 4th November 1895 Eugene Field Sr died in Chicago of a heart attack at the age of 45. He is buried at the Church of the Holy Comforter in Kenilworth, Illinois.

The New York Times described his death: CHICAGO, Nov. 4. — Eugene Field, the poet and humorist, died at 5 o'clock this morning of heart disease at his residence in Buena Park. Although Mr. Field had been ill for the past three days, his sudden death was totally unexpected.

Field was originally interred at Graceland Cemetery in Chicago, but his son-in-law, Senior Warden of the Church of the Holy Comforter, had him reinterred on 7th March, 1926.

Several of his poems were set to music with commercial success. Many of his works were accompanied by paintings from the exceptional talents of Maxfield Parrish.

During his lifetime he was often referred to as the 'poet of childhood'. This may account for his anonymous publication of 'Only a Boy'. In our own times the work would probably be frowned upon. It concerns a 12-year-old boy being seduced by a woman in her 30s. The 1920's drama critic/magazine editor George Jean Nathan claimed it was a popular but forbidden work among those coming of age in the early 1900's.

Much of what Field wrote was light, humourous and of its time. And that is perhaps why it has endured. Its writes of a time that, in his words, suspends itself from the harsh reality of real life to a gentler and more touching time that exists in the imagination.

Eugene Field – A Concise Bibliography

The Tribune Primer (1882)
Culture's Garland (1887)
A Little Book of Profitable Tales (1889)
A Little Book of Western Verse (1889)
With Trumpet and Drum (1892)
Echoes from the Sabine Farm (1893)
The Holy Cross and Other Tales (1893)
Second Book of Verse (1893)
Love Songs of Childhood (1894)
Love Affairs of a Bibliomaniac (1895)
Little Willie (1895)
Songs and Other Verse (1896)
Second Book of Tales (1896)
The House; An Episode in the Lives of Reuben Baker, Astronomer and His Wife Alice (1896)
Field Flowers (1896)
Florence Bardsley's Story (1897)
Lullaby Songs of Childhood (1897)
Lullaby Land (1898)
Sharps and Flats (1900)
The Stars (1901)
Nonsense for Old and Young (1901)
A Little Book of Nonsense (1901)
A Little Book of Tribune Verse (1901)
The Sabine Farm (1903)
John Smith USA (1905)
The Clink of Ice (1905)
Hoosier Lyrics (1905)
Cradle Lullabies (1909)
The Poems of Eugene Field (1910)
Christmas Tales and Christmas Verse (1912)
Penn-Yan Bill's Wooing (1914)
The Yankee Abroad (1917)
The Mouse and the Moonbeam (1919)
Poems of Childhood (1920)

The Gingham Dog and the Calico Cat (1926)
Child Verses (1927)
The Sugar Plum Tree (1929)
In Wink-a-way Land (1930)

www.ingramcontent.com/pod-product-compliance
Lightning Source LLC
Chambersburg PA
CBHW060101050426
42448CB00011B/2572